Premonitions of an Uneasy Guest

Also by Carolyne Wright:

Stealing the Children
Returning What We Owed

PREMONITIONS
OF AN
UNEASY GUEST

by Carolyne Wright

Hardin-Simmons University Press
Abilene, Texas 79698

Acknowledgements

Anthology of Magazine Verse: Early Fall: the Adirondacks

Black Warrior Review: Leaving the Conservatory; Photo of Myself Taken Near the Mission Range

Bloodroot: Separate Drawing Boards

Colorado-North Review: Dream Teller; "Eulene's a nun now. . . ."

Colorado State Review: Eulene; She Talks to Herself About Eulene

Cutbank: Ferry Ride

Denver Quarterly: A High Wind Through Your Life

Fiddlehead: Hard Beauty

Fragments: "Nothing rightly flowers. . . ."

Georgia Review (The): The Mythology of Guns

Intro 10: The Speech of Children

Intro 11: Cyclists' Stop Along Tecumseh Road; Woman and Luna Moth in a Telephone Booth: Late Evening

Jeopardy: Eulene; Pangs of the Moon Coast

Kansas Quarterly: Two Measures

Malahat Review: The Morning Mail: a Brief Irreverie; Early Fall: the Adirondacks

Montana Review: Leaving the House I Grew Up In; "Eulene's letting Salvatore go. . . ."; Homecoming; Leaving the Conservatory

Nimrod: Night Walk Around Green Lakes

Ploughshares: "Mania Klepto"

Plum: Sierra Walk

Poetry (Chicago): Choosing My Name

Poetry Northwest: 613

Poetry Now: Returning What We Owed

Poetry Seattle: Ancestress

Poets On: Vital Connection

Porch: Awakened at 4 A.M. to My Mother's Insomnia By My Brother Playing the Piano

Quarterly West: Indian Woman on Socabaya Street

Slackwater Review: Photo of Myself Taken Near the Mission Range

Stand: Rehearsal for a Visit

Syracuse Scholar: Woman and Luna Moth in a Telephone Booth: Late Evening

The Smith (Pulpsmith): The Mid-Winter Month: a Nightmare; After Harvard Square: Eulene's Bread and Circuses

Writer's Forum 6: Premonitions of an Uneasy Guest; Strange Wintry Country With a Garden

Writer's Forum 8: The Morning Mail: a Brief Irreverie

The following poems appeared in a limited edition chapbook, *Returning What We Owed,* Owl Creek Press, 1980. Copyright 1980 by Carolyne Wright.

Choosing My Name, Leaving the House I Grew Up In, "Mania Klepto," Riding Through Slums, Premonitions of an Uneasy Guest, Ferry Ride, 613, Homecoming, "Eulene's letting Salvatore go. . . .," Leaving the Conservatory, Returning What We Owed.

"The Discipline of Becoming Invisible" appeared previously in *Stealing the Children,* Ahsahta (Boise State University) Press, 1978. Copyright 1978 by Carolyne Wright.

I am grateful to the Millay Colony, The Fine Arts Work Center in Province town, the Dorland Mountain Colony, and the Creative Artist's Public Service Program for their support while this book was being completed.

Special thanks go to all those who have given their encouragement along the way, especially Donald Dike, George P. Elliott, and Yusef Komunyakaa.

Premonitions of an Uneasy Guest, by Carolyne Wright, is published in cooperation with the Associated Writing Programs and is a contribution to the *AWP Series for Contemporary Poetry.*

Library of Congress Catalog Card Number: 82-82221

ISBN: 0-910075-01-8

Hardin-Simmons University Press, Abilene, Texas 79698
Copyright 1983 by Hardin-Simmons University
Printed in the United States of America

Cover photo used by permission of The Mansell Collection, London.

Again, for Marian.

TABLE OF CONTENTS

Acknowledgments

I. *Choosing A Name*   1

Choosing My Name   2
The Morning Mail: a Brief Irreverie   4
Leaving the House I Grew Up In   6
"Mania Klepto"   7
613   9

II. *The Discipline of Becoming Invisible*   11

The Discipline of Becoming Invisible   12
Pangs of the Moon Coast   14
Sierra Walk   15
Indian Woman on Socabaya Street   17
Ancestress   19
Riding Through Slums   20
Strange Wintry Country With a Garden   22
Cyclists' Stop Along Tecumseh Road   23
Night Walk Around Green Lakes   24
The Speech of Children   25
Returning What We Owed   26

III. *Eulene*   27

Eulene   29
"Eulene is troubled. . . ."   31
She Talks to Herself About Eulene   32
Dream Teller   33
The Mid-Winter Month: a Nightmare   34
On Vacation with Eulene   35
Eulene's Hallowe'en   36
After Harvard Square: Eulene's Bread and Circuses   37
"Eulene's letting Salvatore go. . . ."   38
"Eulene's a nun now. . . ."   39

IV. *Premonitions of an Uneasy Guest*   41

    Ferry Ride   43
    Separate Drawing Boards   44
    Homecoming   46
    Rehearsal for a Visit   48
    Early Fall: the Adirondacks   49
    Premonitions of an Uneasy Guest   50
    Woman and Luna Moth in a Telephone Booth: Late Evening   51

V. *Vital Connections*   53

    Vital Connection   55
    Two Measures   56
    Awakened at 4 A.M. to My Mother's Insomnia
     By My Brother Playing the Piano   57
    Little Rock Mission   58
    "Nothing rightly flowers...."   59
    Dictating the Answers   60
    The Mythology of Guns   62
    A High Wind Through Your Life   63
    Leaving the Conservatory   65
    Hard Beauty   66
    Photo of Myself Taken Near the Mission Range,
     Montana: Early Summer, 1974   67

"Everything is yielding toward a forgone conclusion.
Only we are rash enough to go on changing our lives."
—Adrienne Rich, "The Blue Ghazals"

Choosing A Name

Choosing My Name

Start with the givens: strong artisan,
gleaned from Marian Bible lists
and definitions out of Random House,
what the strained sires slapped on me
when the surgeon banged my behind
into song. Law and custom urge me
to observe them, take notes, protect them
under my rummage sale camouflages
in all seasons. I train the syllables
on the anonymous skin till I forget
how often names fall short before
the exposed face of a thought.

In the clearings between signatures
that flourish like ancestral foliage
on letters home, I still glimpse
legions marching over cloudy Gaul,
blunt churls in leather aprons
tapping the clumsy Saxon shoes.
What would I choose, if I had
my own way, closer to the pulse?
Loose wool spun to fine hard thread
on spools? A pause between rains?
A brave crouched in a sweathouse
waiting for a root to point a finger,
hard eyes opening in the crooks of trees,
an ancient ruffed grouse beating
its true name out in a last, oracular
stutter? The choices fight each other
like boys having it out at last
in a closing elevator.

If I had my way,
there'd be no explaining. The round
letters could sprawl or clatter
in square boxes, no one would throw
a sound back like a fish too small,
folks wouldn't rummage their minds
for old tags as for a loose sock's double.
Can one new penny, tooth, or Christmas
of a name help? Most come to their conclusions
as a tired bum to a stoop, stop
at the first syllable the finger lands on.
The attendance lists drone on, John after John.
What can we do in a language
where saints are praised
but pessimists are more authentic?

The Morning Mail: a Brief Irreverie

I get invitations—form letters
with my name filled in
from mail order guest lists.
I read them at bulk rate
before the trash can closes
my subscription. I riffle through
the well-digested readers, the endless
once-a-lifetime offers, the self-thumping
Bible kits, to set straight the states
and kingdoms I've seceded from.
I've run too many business rounds,
scratching tasks off lists
like lice off a rabbit.

Meanwhile, a surveilling eye
on a retractable stalk peers at me
from all directions. It's taking notes:
digits click off behind its retina
like gambling slots. Satisfied,
it pulls back to its box
and snaps the lid down.
                                    I get up,
knock the egg shells from my plate,
and wait—not for the clock
to bong out doom, nor for my ride,
its ancient Goodyears rubbing
white caulk on the curb—but for the eyes
that glare from the papering
as I leave the room.

What have I done to earn such coverage?
What Cerberus lurks at my gates,
a dog in postman's clothing?
Could I sneak by, just once,
all watchers but the single eye—I,
a refugee of blindfolds
in a world at large?

Leaving the House I Grew Up In

The sea squid on the hatrack
wriggles its tentacles in my face.
I can't hang up my sou'wester
without being wrapped in an eight-armed
embrace. But I forgive: its writhing's
calisthenic, and it, too, poor hanger-on,
flounders out of place here.
It's the knick-knack shelves I must avoid,
the fusty old victrolas, the lace
antimacassars that jostle each other
for the parlor air. It's underwater-thick
with dust in here, and a fly that gave up
on the glass pane long ago
drones dully.
        If I thought,
All this house needs
is a mummy that falls from the closet
like a fold-out ironing board, my folks
would get it, putting two more revolutions
in their circular account. But I waive
my power of suggestion
for a stronger cure: Three dawns
a week, I duck the long reek
that hangs in middle air—the ghost
of a cigar—and hand-and-knee it
out the grillwork door.

The tentacles fall off me then
like tarred rope from a mooring,
and I pick up my life again—
light's daughter making her allotted
progress, hungry for the sun's
refractions through the glass,
those dawning spectra that fan out
along the far shores of her childhood
like a promise almost forgotten.

"Mania Klepto"

You never come to shoplift
but to leave things: rhinestone
butterflies you borrowed
from mother's vanity, assorted
lengths of nails, your brother's
manic metronome that ticks in its box
like the crocodile in Peter Pan.
You have to be discreet and furtive
as a Gideon Bible placement clerk,
dart your hand out when the eyes
in the back of the store detective's
head blink. You place each object
so it says, "I've always been here,"
blends into the merchandise
like a wallflower.
                              Petty generosity
made up the family litany,
dinned so long in your ear
you never could forget it,
even between birthdays.
You've spent years trying
to be normal—a taker of tickets
and free rides, the gifts and creatures
of sucker friends' philanthropy. Now
you know better, the mania so familiar
it's conviction. You go through the motions
like a master evangelist, breaking into
fertile grounds for quick drops
and quicker getaways, subtle Appleseeder
of an excess of possessions. How else
could anyone receive them?

You no longer question, merely smile
at the racks of garments, the thin
bored women who assess them.
You deposit the last dress you've brought,
calm-faced and professional as a mannikin.
The dressing room corridor turns
into a Valhalla of mirrors, and you—
Dame Quixote armed only with a bare
bent hanger—finally contend with the grim
glass-multiplied reflections.

613

Never bring your elbows to this class.
There's barely room to duck the dean's eye
coming at you like a clammy funhouse hand.
You wake up at dawn, love nailed high
on your list of intentions, remind yourself
to hold your blood's calls in abeyance
till the right bells ring, get to class
on time.
        This time, we learn how
to manipulate the inside views—words
that have heard of each other,
ridden up elevators together,
never yet been introduced. You try
to remember what comes after How Are You.
But it's a damp fuse,
and the omniscient author's prose
monotonous as the barroom conquests
in the late late show.
              You doze.
Lovers drift side-by-side in your thoughts
like leaves on a river.
You peel off superlatives like clothes,
the dream stands up to repeated readings,
there's not one adjective to edit.

You start; it's over. The class falls out
like a regiment—the same show of feet,
meters winding down in all the faces,
briefcases tight with thoughts
too stuffy to admit they've met.
Left out, like a student from one
of those small, angry countries, you see
your best harangues have dwindled,
sunk to footnotes in some rival text.
Even old lovers, whose best moans
quote yours, keep the credit.

A secret zero
starts its slow growth in your heart.
It will look for allies everywhere.

The Discipline of Becoming Invisible

The Discipline of Becoming Invisible

The discipline of becoming invisible
is not what you think it is.
Start by driving all night
cross-country, avoiding towns.
Travel light: take breath,
words enough for a few poems,
your clearest sight.
Don't calculate the miles
or wonder if you'll ever get to the point
on the map where your road
breaks off.
                You can't miss invisibility;
it wears your face
inside out. It stares back at you
everywhere:
                It's on the signs at midnight
glowing off the shoulder of the road.
It's in the number of hours
and the sleep it takes
to drain a city out of you.
It's in the light that fires
your retinas with sight.

When you arrive at the tollgate
where the road ends,
you'll pay the last of yourself
out, as the roped nerves
uncoil themselves
from the base of your brain.
Invisibility will be your change;
you'll realize you've carried it
all the way, like chromosomes
or the life maps on your palms.

Now, when you peer into the rear-
view mirror, only the road
winds backward in the glass distance.
As you slide away—into the high,
clairvoyant blue of dusk—
you'll wonder what sign it was,
in what unknown code at the road's edge,
first glowed in your sleep
and pointed here,
                where your breath lets go,
and your sight opens
as it turns to light.

Pangs of the Moon Coast

Trying to sleep, we left
our true selves at the far end
of the rain. Lessons
we should have learned
stayed folded, fears for safety
that did not unclench.
We stepped to one side
of the dream to get here:
Front door, a strange family
whose first glance
decided how we dressed.
Younger sisters knew
we harbored foreign gods
like illicit cargoes.
A huge city hovered
over us like the echo
of a frown. We took our exit—
passengers who boarded the wrong
idea—and backtracked, fishing
imitation fortune cookies
from our pockets.

The full moon dropped over the edge,
cheap mirror in a hand
anxious to please.
The old distress invaded, gliding in
over the coastline of our sleep.
Deep in the fenced runs of our ears
the dogs barked till morning.
Ancestors bristled around us
like bare trees in the wrong season.
Before dawn, visions detached themselves
from our retinas and walked around,
leaving hieroglyphic warnings
on the lintels, all our entrances
and exits under guard.

Sierra Walk

(Ollantaitambo, Perú)

The Inca woman trudges ahead
on the rutted llama track,
her silence dark and tightly
braided. Above us, eucalyptus
limbs hold up the night.

An hour ago, when
I stepped off the Cuzco-
Machu Picchu local, the thin air
reeled with constellations.
I asked the way to town.
The station master swung his oil
lamp, and our smudged faces
flickered on its panes.

No, he didn't know the roads,
the platform's widening rings
of dark. He never held in mind
what dropped away over the edges
of a white man's sight.
"But this *cholita*," he pointed
to a shape bent under bundles
and layers of shawls, "can take you.
They all know the way."

The woman assented in a warble
high and strange as a candle
flicker in a mountain shrine.
She turned and walked. I
took my pack and followed.

Other shapes fall in behind,
stocky and silent as my guide.
I shift the pack's unbalanced
load, shrink into layers
of my own dark. Among forms
that fit the path—like priests
in whatever road their god
guides them—I must save myself
from stumbling.

Oil lamps in windows
fix our silhouettes. The road
turns into town. In the square
the crowd disbands, lamps go down
like lids. The Inca woman
moves up the mountain
to her hut of fitted stone.

I move alone through the streets,
speechless, dark as faces
extinguished under shawls,
trying to empty myself of all names
and summon the courage
to knock on windowless plank doors
and ask the blank-faced dwellers
for a room.

Indian Woman on Socabaya Street
(Potosí, Bolivia)

She squats on the corner,
a cud of coca
wadded in one cheek.
She spins a spool of wool
in and out of her fingers,
the center in a wheel
of skirts. Onions in baskets
and bowls filled with corn gruel
at her feet. Shrug
of her shawl to ward off my eye
and she's faceless.
A padded alpaca hump. Whatever
the inside of a stone thinks
must shine in her.

(Faint bulbs strung in a mine
glow on hands sorting
over the moving belts. Fingers
blink across the tin. The bulbs
swing as a rumble dawns
deep in the rock.
The glow on fingers
stutters as the roof falls in,
dark as shawls
pitched over the sun.)

She speaks to me
in a tongue guttural as lead.
A creased hand paws my pocket.
I gesture, I have nothing.
Her eyes flint hard
against mine, she spits out her name
for me with a curse
and laughs. What she invokes
turns the corner with me.

That night, my dreams file
like miners from their shafts,
carrying the old words
knotted in sisal, gold masks
from faces with no memories.
In abandoned cities,
five-hundred-year-old echoes
catch up to their cries.
Over the high ranges, axes
go up and down. Strange
hands loosen on the stone.

Ancestress

She climbs the stairs slowly,
a grand old lady, stares out
stained windows at the frozen
garden, ties edged ribbons in
the stray hairs of the day.

Not much is left of the old ways.
After the children moved out,
the secret halls and corridors
seemed to go on forever
in all directions, a forgotten maze.

The many-generationed family
had learned perfectly the art
of discreet evasion. Every time
a butler passed, a door jamb
offered itself, or a Persian drapery,

or a deep bay window. "Hide here,"
they whispered. "The others never look,
never imagine anything foreign
creeping in. It's always afternoon
here, always prosperous and between wars,

always dust-free where the sun falls."
Alone, her life runs down, clock left
in a vacant room, her mind reshelving
each thought, librarian at closing.
Forgotten questions pay their calls

as the afternoon sinks to its knees
and light leans toward the far edge
of the fields like a child over a ledge:
"What does the blood say?" "Silence, please."
"The breath, bird's voice?" "The trees, the trees!"

Riding Through Slums

Riding into wintry Connecticut,
between houses boarded up like faces
guarding their dreams, lights out
in the bus as if that wrapped asbestos

around the roar, we stretch stiffening legs
out among old schedules, sandwich bags,
and the newsprint-blackened floor. How did
the mayflies of our expectations make it

past the first block with their wings still on?
The squat rowhouses toil up the hill;
mill wives line up at the bus stops for children
who spill out the doors like coal slag, all

yells and brittle edges. Brownstone faces
discourage guests: our eyes. Mildew is
taking over the family businesses.
Backyard pools harden to ice,

lozenges stuck in grim plastic wrappers.
What did we hope for? The most flypaper question.
No toil-varicosed arms open for us, strangers,
free-thinking in our queer dialect of green:

landscaped gardens and polished, perfect flowers.
Not even the school vansful of children,
pounding on the glass for our attention
and whooping till their bus roar is the louder,

would understand the clipped lawns in our chatter.
We must make our peace with gray, with brown,
no matter what state—New Hampshire,
Jersey, or despair—we're in. Our plan

will be private, anarchic, subject to whim or fits
of weather; will adapt to flight or sudden noises.
Until we find it, we'll ride through darkening streets,
thankful for every gap between houses.

Strange Wintry Country With a Garden

I
Always the sensation of new life
riding through forests with the windows
down, remote mansions flickering
like candles through the trees.
We surge with Christmasses.

II
A branch breaks off. Green veins
bleed into air. All the passers-
by in the garden pause, a sudden
frost of a stare. A fruit
lets go of its stem, its bruising
plump in turf muffled.
The scene turns over like a leaf
before it falls, sleepers
almost awakening. Their hearts—
stone gardens raked by stooped,
obedient men at dawn.

III
Traffic at a distance mimics geese,
slow wheeling around of the long flocks.
Pale green pries through our lids.
We turn under the heaped snow
of the blankets, searching again
in the back alleys of sleep
for wind that whistles thinner
as if through a shrinking reed.
Dreams recede, kettles ringing
at winter's borders, stones
over old ice that skip and startle
before they plunge. Our lids
fly up, alarmed. That's all. Morning
comes into focus on the wall.

Cyclists' Stop Along Tecumseh Road

We stop, throw our gear down in fallow-land.
We stare into the sky's unbroken blue
until it swarms with photons: alchemists'
gold gnats of light. We'd like to drop
what weights us—books, proofs of identity,
centuries of kneeling to the untransmuted god
of fact—and stride into that blue pacific
barely furrowed by cumulus' wide prows.

But cedars lean over the pasture,
shadows rest like cold fingers on us.
It's too late to go against the slope
of fields, the dimming magnitude
of sun; too late to do more than bow
to the light green shimmering around
the leaves' veined green, try once more
to coax their medicine, listen to yarrow
and chamomile murmur their properties
over the locusts' swelling drone.

The crowd of sweet clovers nods heads
in assent: everywhere the underleaf,
the brown swell of water. Wild carrot
closes down its simple manufacture
for the night. A beetle, burnished
as opal, tumbles off its clover
when we touch it, into the lengthening
sleep of the field.
              We shiver
in the green chill, and pedal back
to our four walls—our self-made element—
and dream all night of heat lightning
gathering its forces, glimmering
from one horizon to the other of our sleep.

Night Walk Around Green Lakes

Above Hancock Field, light keeps on
arriving in stars' past formations.
Late jets circle in the holding
patterns, Syracuse glows over the horizon
like a dying sun. The engines' roar
lags behind, cone of a noise
pointed backwards: silence,
landing lights advancing on the night.
Silence, too, where the Pleiades,
misty sisters, huddle under
the sky's dome, where the ancients
watched huge gladiators wheel
and stride down the dark ecliptic.
At midnight, the jewels in Orion's belt
glitter through the smog.

Let's ask the few owls left
for wisdom, save some inflections
from the clipped shriek of a mouse.
When we go, we take our tail lights
with us: fuel exhaust streaming
behind us like Andromeda's veil.
As if Diogenes, old Cynic,
had thrust his lamp into our faces,
left us dazed; then stumped away,
hefting his receding light,
we slam the car doors, shift into
position, turn out of the driveway.
All night, the Great Bears
circle each other in the sky.

The Speech of Children

In this dream, you understand the speech
of children—shy, sibilant, its meaning
poised at the edges of your own.
You loom, a large uneasy branch above them.
The children smile and twist their fingers;
their faces bloom into yours and give
the sudden ripe fruit of their seeing.
Later, waking into the blue hesitance
of morning, you remember something
that felt mother to you, far down
the corridor of sleep. You step out,
onto the concrete walk you've laid,
and notice the faces of other houses,
their thoughts shuttered—adults pacing
back and forth in the upstairs rooms,
wondering what it was that drove off
while they slept, erasing its passing
like print of a book they no longer believe in.

Returning What We Owed

The first tracks we came upon were those
of old digressions. Not only did our scent
cover them, but other animals had littered
the clearings with their various sleeps.
After that, migrations south drew us,
or branches starting suddenly from fog,
or stems straightening like spinal columns
to push up to light. Deers' browsing
tracks crisscrossed in the burdock;
only our hearts stood like stone markers
old scouts laid. Finally, the green
of semper vivens receding toward snow line
persuaded us beyond what we already knew.
What we loved we left in hand-hewn shelters
by the trail. Whole lives—all we trusted—
would have to pick up where we left them,
returning what they owed us in that taking.
Meanwhile, we, like travellers
in Sesshu scrolls, had waded through
the rapids, gone around the last bend
anyone could guess at from the road.

Eulene

Eulene

I have to give up coffee.
Eulene tosses and turns all night
and I get up in the morning
black and blue and twisted.

My dreams give me a cramp in the throat
when I try to laugh.
Eulene

is the blank-faced onlooker
in all those dreams.
The only thing she will say to me is
"Don't give me away."

Everytime I try to sketch Eulene
she slides behind my back.
I can't stop her hands
from reaching around to pick
at the hairs on my chin.

Sometimes I feel like putting Eulene
in an elevator and pushing
the down button. Let her go
to the sub-basement.
She could make a living there,
putting the lids on dreams.

Then she'd be safe.
My hands have tried to strangle her
too many times in dreams,
but she's always jumped out the window
just in time.

Now that I'm awake,
I ought to finish off this last cup
of coffee, and throw
the dregs in the trash.

Maybe then I could go downstairs
and pull the lids off.

Eulene will never notice.
Not until I shake a bag
of dead birch leaves
on the floor where she throws her fits,
leave her the garbage and the dirty cups,
and go outside for good.

"Eulene is troubled. . . ."

Eulene is troubled.
There's no way we can be in the same room
with other people anymore.
When my lover walks in,
he puts down his briefcase and afternoon,
and we sit in silence
till the workday tick-tock of our thinking
deepens, We ignore Eulene, of course,
and she flounces out the door,
as loud as platform heels and dark green
nail gloss and aggressive bubblegum can take her.
But no one's listening now.
Not even me.
Just my nerve ends twinging a little
as they feel for the absence
and the dragon's teeth in the smile
she's taking down the stairs,
and the shamed face I should be glad to lose.

She Talks to Herself About Eulene

Eulene's getting funky again,
bad actress in a Passion Play.
Just when you thought she was
too old for the goodtimers
who run out on her each weekend.
Haven't you learned that Eulene
will make excuses, talk to mirrors,
wishing for her own coin
to drop into the eye-wells?
She'll wear red tights, cruise
for everyday men in the park,
take apart the telephone to find
what makes it ring. She knows
no one watches closely anymore.
Tie her hair back. Make her listen
to the songs whose meanings
unravel in her blood. You haven't found out
how deep the cup is
you must drink, or if,
when you set it down, it breaks
desire's bad connection.
How can you know then—when Eulene
slams her door at night—who's
at attention? You, so in love by now
you have to sleep alone.

Dream Teller

In Eulene's dreams there's a teller
in a barred window who tallies the figures
and sends back the statement
in the morning. He knows Eulene
too well, knows how she fudges
on the balance. He's laid it on the line
too many times for her to mislay
what he means, but still the dreams
don't come out even.
Instead, they balk, back up,
and get stuck in sleep's keyhole
like ransom notes. Eulene's always missed
the rented angels standing at attention in them,
big and beef-faced as policemen.
She thinks they're sales clerks,
smiles pulling their mouths wide as toads',
pointing with sticky prehensiles
to the One Thing She Really Wants.
But she can't see around them, see
the other sides blinking like Christmas pendants
in the turning light. She lets herself
be gulled so well she never knows.
And they never tell.

When Eulene wakes up, there's no one
to get even with.
Just a red light flashing on and off and on
above the teller's booth.
Outside, the morning drives away
on its official round.
Eulene's left standing there,
crumpled stubs of her canceled passbook
clutched tight in her hand.

The Mid-Winter Month: a Nightmare

Eulene's mind
is the infinite distance of mid-winter
from mine.
On the laboratory window,
behind which she formulates some law,
her breath-steam seals over
into ice. Outside,
my fingers, purpled,
scrape it to the raw.

Eulene's a plant researcher;
she clamps electrodes
to the green, tranquil nerves,
and switches on the thoughts
of her machines. Their oscillograph lines
scrawl out shock after shock after shock.
There's no way in words I can stop her.

Before darkness hardens over me,
I'm going to run from Eulene
into the green of my own distance.
No dial gauged to pain
will root me out, and Eulene
will paralyze into a chemist's coat,
bent over beakers white with frozen steam
from her frozen throat.

On Vacation with Eulene
(Wreck Cove, Nova Scotia)

Over-weighted we've come, under the fog,
taking on a North Atlantic wind
long after the others fall asleep.
I shiver and decode Vallejo
while Eulene hunches into her bad mood
like a turtle's neck,
and plucks out eyelashes
                         one
by one. "Why?" I ask, but she keeps
her mouth shut, as usual.

When will she finally shirk
the perfectionist's punishment—
the picking and plucking and push push push—
and look wide open in my eyes?
"That's the road," she says,
then makes detour after detour
of excuses not to. It's the terrible joy
of swerving that makes Eulene grab at the wheel.

"Let go," I tell myself, when Eulene takes off
with her weight and the counterfeiting
of her smile. "If she walks out
without her slicker on, the Gesundheitgeist
that grabs at her won't snare your breath.
Her clockwork God ticks off
each lash that falls. In the morning,
He'll burn off her fog."

All's well, the nuclear code
throbs under all denials.

Eulene's Hallowe'en

Eulene's a shunpiker,
but her lovely meanders get less lovely
farther down the road, and the toll's
inflation's geometric on each deviant inch.
Take Hallowe'en, just as a for-instance:
All the death-wish heads were glued
like flies to the wallpaper, and Eulene,
got up in sari and clown white,
glided to the graveyard
with her household's other wraiths.
What could she do there, but play
tombstone leapfrog and let out
midnight's pumpkin-colored shrieks?
Her obeisance with folded hands
was a posture for no friends, and her best pal
Salvatore was in Osh-Kosh, hillbilly slouch,
and belch. They'd never match.
At home, one plain, unJack-o-Lanterned candle
spilled twelve threads of wax—time
to get off the boneyard's muddy tracks.
But Salvatore had disappeared
with a carbon-compound wizard
and a wraith.
                    Give up that applebob,
Eulene: even in mask and costume
you walk home alone.

After Harvard Square:
Eulene's Bread and Circusses

What a smattering of culture Eulene's got.
A chopstick here, a tatter of Punjabi
cotton there, and on her walls,
the latest in the Vorpal market's art.
Conducing, all of it, to what?
Not to the overpopulation of the heart,
or to the string-twangings
of the popular affectioners;
not, surely, to "Gimme lo-ove, LOVE!"
No. Eulene stalks down the street, her eyes
burning the whole show thin,
her mind's hands knocking out
the flim-flam frames that prettify
life's knuckled force.
Sometimes she strays,
ghosting past the copy rooms
where they plug salvation into stereos . . .

Until she remembers the bare walls
of the heart, a sea wind
through the open door, and the salt-
water sun whose first light
splashes on the spotless floor.

"Eulene's letting Salvatore go. . . ."

Eulene's letting Salvatore go,
dropping the ropes off. After all,
he never was a grand piano, or a safe
being lowered from the thirty-seventh floor.
Just a boy trying to be holy
without the seamless tunic or the wings,
making everyone else's aureole go dim.
He had to be the saint with the most gold leafing
in the room. Eulene was spoiling him,
patting his curly head and taking his arm
as if they really were as warm as friends.
"But it's cold the flyway that I'm on,
and I'm going north this fall,"
he said. That's why he won't relent
under affection, but looks straight on,
a stern V of eyebrows.
                              Eulene knows now
that love's more than a tail hypnotized with salt,
or a figleaf and muscles on a pedestal,
or even the glow that let's her see
the angels' wings: Love's driving her
to robes and rosaries and the blood
that pulses through that glow.
                              Salvatore knows.
That's why he turns his head away,
why no doves teeter on the stem behind his eyes.
Besides, he's never let himself fall low enough
to kneel beside her where she prays.

"Eulene's a nun now...."

Eulene's a nun now,
kneeling in her college room.
Unvowed still, and unvestmented, she dares
to call the winter sun down on her house.
Let it sear away the hashish smells,
dog stains in the hallway. That bummer,
memory, building its nests in the drawers.
Let it burn into the beer-bleared eyes
averted when Eulene walks in. Fears
that roll the sleeping bags tighter
behind Venetian blinds. Bullies
who look for victims in the mirrors.
Eulene packs her only change
of clothes, peels the labels
from her judgement jars,
the fist in her ribcage
clenching and unclenching.
She's signed her soul up
for a job: quick-change artists
moving in next door,
escape routes into the country
cordoned off.

Premonitions of an Uneasy Guest

Ferry Ride

Puget Sound, Washington

The great return boat glides past ours,
a red kite on an invisible wire
fluttering behind it like an afterthought,
the kite flyer hidden in a leeward
shelter from the stiffening breeze.
We move between islands, the water
a blue field ferries plow, the mainland
dark with hemlocks wrapped in their boughs
like monks in winter. We glance
from the prow at the lowering sun,
our shadows lengthening behind us.
Buoys bob hard in the darkening channels
of our thinking—warnings breaking
the water's flat sheen, the easy glide
of speech. Caution's invisible wires
tug at the words that flag out
of our silence. The truth is locked up
in us—what preserves our lives.

We stare hard at the darkening water,
the wheeling flocks of gulls,
and when we're honest, at each other.
Like the engines that throb
below decks, driving the boat
into the night, we've moved toward,
then across each other—glintings
on the ridges of the rip tides,
the ferry's subsiding wake.

We've locked in the dark
between moons, our bodies lingering
on their own peculiar meanings;
then given ourselves to our differing sleeps—
our lives, in dream, two rows of lights
winking off a long pier toward the sea.

Separate Drawing Boards

The old Mexican dozes on the bus,
his head in his old wife's lap.
They've been making love in Spanish
all their lives. We roll past
alfalfa fields, head lettuce in rows,
the slow turning of the sprinklers' arms.
Farther out, beyond the buttes,
the land rises, dries, tufts into sagebrush.
I don't need any excuse to look out the window,
gaze at the couples as they shift and doze,
let my hands reach for sage blooms
in the arroyos. You're not in the landscape.

When the mind glances toward you,
it blinds suddenly like an eye
staring head-on at the sun;
sees, in its reeling, only the spot,
memory's blue after-image.
Nowhere a clear picture, nowhere
the draughtsman's lamp turned
on the illustration boards,
landscapes we brushed deftly
onto paper, dark from light, with #4
sables and our sense of what was right,
what fit the composition.

Only the scene
that glides by out the window,
farther and farther from the mattes we cut
to frame the pictures labelled "Us"—
you, several states behind me, and I,
with no idea of what town's next,
or what will come of the life we've played at,
pencils not yet sharpened for the visions
that drive me eastward, where
the highway divides over our blank,
respective drawing boards.

Homecoming

I'll come back dry-eyed from vacation,
back to business: Seattle and what suits it,
gray. Once I said I'd like to move out
on myself, return to find the premises
swept and empty. The usual parable—
the shabby spirits, panicked at the exit
of old thoughts, try to sneak back
with the new, vying with me to pay
seven times the rent.
                 I'll give in,
sublet the nightmare dwellings
to their familiar occupants,
jettison expectations, self-
addressed, enveloped thinking;
and race my shadow for the exit.

Grant me a few moments for the givens,
those gifts wrapped in chameleon skin:
You'll be there, alert and nervous
as a horse's ears, your voice
clinging to mine from the far end
of the line.
            I'll say, Out there
the road took unexpected detours,
crossed bridges you can't get to
from the highway. My own reflection
was complete. I grew unexacting
in my touch as air, made love
a matter of kissing
and letting well enough alone.

                    You'll reply,
I dreamed safety into the arm's-length
of your letters, learned how dusk lingers
under hemlocks, tried to be loyal.
And me: Loyalty, that leaning of the heart,
indeed. Can we give each other
what we really need?

I'll give what I've brought—
miles of roadway, long walks
under broad-leafed shade, words
beating at my head with urgent wings,
a new kindness learned when a man's
failing love stirred me: private joys
that give us back to ourselves, friends
showing each other the gentle way out.

Rehearsal for a Visit

Known in advance: the slalom's curves,
the skier's muscles mirroring the course.
The twinge at each gate 's as familiar
as the key's click in your door.
Your door: the press-down letters say
"I'd rather not be changed." The touched up
touch-me-not new paint job, the look
of wanting to back out before thé argument's
resolved. In the storeroom, canvasses
stretched and gessoed into consequence.
I could tell you the directions
your possessions point. If there is
another world, dear, it's in this one.
I've dragged that fingernail long enough
across your sleep.
                    Goodbye. Stop by, perhaps,
before I take the next boat out:
Look back at the rough wake we left,
what skiffs' thin hulls heave over.
What else to do, years from what stills
our longing, when the only sane thing
is to love? What heals us, stronger
than any substitutes our brushes
rough out: years of shade the leafy afternoons
sneak in through our dreams' back doors.
Gone, I promise to keep clean, alert,
dart out before my heart caves in—
one jump ahead of the Spirit.

Early Fall: The Adirondacks

Our private foliage has unscrolled
all summer, drifted imperceptibly
as oak leaves into fall, the burnt
red edges of a need. Around
the thickest trunks, the hopeful
start their raking. They overturn
the broken stems of older,
failed seasons.
                    Now, aster
and wild carrot flourish
in the deep space of the meadows
like widening clouds of stars,
and slashes of early foliage
leap at the eye from shadows
grinding out longer and longer
across the afternoon.
                    How many times
have we known this, outfitted ourselves
for departure, turned within our well-
oiled parts on the slanting axis
of the season? Now I would ask,
in the chill these higher altitudes
bring out, how is it that we've come
this far? What makes us stumble
over our own hope as if over a root
split off suddenly at a switchback?
What will we do with the truth
when it finally arrives: a season,
a sculpture marching clean and finished
from the stone, a light coming steadily
through an interstellar mist?

Premonitions of an Uneasy Guest

The landscape has quietly rearranged itself
while you slept. Mists lying low
along the field bottoms have wandered off,
shaking their spectral heads
like befuddled guests after a party.
The tamaracks have scattered their green lace
and made a dark fugue from the forest.
They line up now outside the front gate
as if for a handout. Even mushrooms,
those sturdy colonists of the late rains,
have clustered in their rubbery suits
to keep off the dew. Their brown necks
and sou'westers clutter the lawn.

You wake from troubled dreams:
swallow chicks cheeping their panicky
demands, the nest under the eaves
prying loose in a rising wind.
You discover, in dawn's after-silence,
that the world, unstable on its axis,
has transposed itself into a fretful
season: The nest has fallen,
the tamaracks drop brittle needles
on the garden, the wind goes on
rising against the departing mist.
After all you were going to risk—
balancing on a rickety scaffolding
to reaffix that nest—your lover's arms
have crept around the waists
of other dreams, his ambitions packed up
and travelled down the valley.
You find yourself an uneasy guest
in an abandoned cottage no longer
under the carefully directed glance
of anyone you trust.

Woman and Luna Moth in a Telephone Booth: Late Evening

The eyes on the wings stare back at her,
dark-ringed, haunting as the kohl-
rimmed eyes of young wives
in the Coptic mummy portraits.

She has come here to make a call
to a part of her life
that may no longer answer.

The moth clings with its furred legs
to the burn-scored edge
of the telephone table, its wings
brittle, two flakes of parchment.

She is trying to compose a message
that contains as much of the truth
as she knows.

Perhaps the green booth light
echoes the shadows under spring leaves,
the green bark to which it clung,
a pupa in a loosening cocoon.

She swallows; she drops a dime in the slot.
It clatters into the coin box.

The moth shudders for the first time.
Its elaborate antennae fan the air,
scanning for signals in a code so ancient
only the portraits of Coptic wives repeat it.

The voice at the other end of the line
wants her again, agrees with anything,
anything she says. . . .

The moth grips the table's edge
and trembles.

Vital Connections

Vital Connection

When you walk in, the walls
recollect their windows.
Articles on the gadget counters
line up at attention. No one notices
the tape reels turning on the far wall,
the secret we've left unrecorded
until now.
           Between us, friend,
there's a vital connection.
How do you say it? Where the lives
splice, where we go beyond
the sound stage to the pure idea,
dare we utter it: love?
In our own good timing,
we're headed for the same prayer.
Meanwhile, we'll leave it to the spider
plants to creep down the shelves
on their runners, our toothbrushes
to find each other in the dark.
We'll keep our hands in, play
the audience into its own hands.
till the heavy makeup wears thin
and some few take their chances.

They'll pay, just as we did—
nomads for the spirit, driving
our respective back roads toward
what we knew was not your average
turn-of-the-dial station,
but home: a world
where dreams speak in our tongues
and wages are coming.

Two Measures

Your voice has a fat bottom to it.
I swim like a fish out of water.
You hold down the high notes
so the goblets won't shatter.
Off the high dive, I hang forever
in the air. You drive down to Denver,
land a good job square on the carpet:
singing to keep the cocktail hour
within measure. In the lap lanes,
the backstrokers' arms turn
slowly, like paddle wheelers.
I flap and sputter, making
a metrical issue of my belly flops.
You open your throat and belt it,
high glider pulling all the stops.

Awakened at 4 A.M. to My Mother's Insomnia By My Brother Playing the Piano

Your son's arpeggio machine still plays
the same Chopin scherzo evening after evening.
The hall fills with your thoughts.
They make you clutch the collar
of your robe and mutter, "Relax,
read a little, at least *she* isn't up yet."

I hear you fumble for a cigarette,
close the door, and riffle through your books
till dawn. The green reading lamp
gleams on your throat,
until your head finally falls back,
sun jabbing through the long rip
in the curtain. Fretting you
to sleeplessness, I'm wide awake.

              Why the same fears,
like a fugue's theme, coming back?
Every second counts against a lack of love—
your shadow falling with a great weight
on my foot, I drag my heels to forgive.
In dream's rehearsals, your fingers
reach from their pages for my throat.

Someday, mother, may the score between us
be played, may we sleep through the pianist's
all-night etudes, the scales in which dark weighs
us: roamers in cold halls, seeking rest.

Little Rock Mission

The townsfolk know the river's
full of fish, and so it is.
No licenses or limits, Just the fish
that rise to their thinking
and, obedient, bite. By nine
all's quiet at the shopping center.
Down the closed-off boulevards
not one car passes.
Once, a screen door slams.
Crickets reel in their songs,
then one-by-one drone on.

In the black part of town
they laugh hard, throw open
the doors of the storefronts.
That's where we walk.
Past broken stoops, dogs
nosing old nets and tackle.
"Here come them sisters again.
Evenin', sisters."
"Evening."

By the time we start back
at the six blocks' end, faces
at every window. Outside
our skins, the mind's hands
find each other. We slip back
under oak shadows, down the quiet
street. New fish
fill the river to the brim.

"Nothing rightly flowers...."

Nothing rightly flowers without Mary.
What takes the berry by surprise
or makes the thoughts leap in deer's
eyes? What gives the willow back to itself
from the lake's still surface? Her breath
—that moth's wing at my ear—
almost answers. Her mind, in mine
like a hand held in a hand, tells me
"Follow your eye until it leaps a country,
let joy open in your body like the mouths
of cells, string your dream lights up
until men's houses acquiesce
and the constellations step forth
from the twilight
to volunteer their fire.
My sap will straighten up your stem,
graft the strewn twigs of your instants
to my strongest branch...."
                    What other seasons
could I claim but hers? What possible lives
might greet me, like driftwood
washed to my doorstep in the night?

Dictating the Answers

How can the season collapse
so fast? The body falls
back into itself. Outside,
the solstice veers toward
a window shivered with ice—
what's left of our politeness,
the demurred face of moonlight.

Your hands fumble for a book.
The fool Quixote tilts
in his entitled place—a mirrored
hall only a brain manacled
in North African malaria
could scheme.
                    Why our private
references, the moon that drops
to the horizon? Why telephones
ringing late nights—once,
never again? Why—as light arrives
on deer's pasterns through May
leaves—an abrupt, sheer
Everest of the heart?

Laughter drifts upstairs
like a ghost seeking a keeper.
Can one moment in a narrow
infinity of lies
preserve us? Of all terms,
does only We include You,
every other pronoun a denial?

You turn the undeciphered
pages, your face full of mirrors.
We look at each other
across the room, the dark sides
of two moons. The test
is to stare straight on at the Sphinx
and dictate answers to the riddles.

The Mythology of Guns

The rifle's beside you
like a lover
when I crawl into bed.
The barrel gleams in the dark,
an acceptable emotion.
Boxes of ammo shells
by the nightstand are unconditional
terms for love.

Your aim's not calculated,
not a bargain struck with a father
training his misaligned sights
on you, cocking the hammer
of his numbered days,

but your personal myth—
the basement stocked with survival
rations for a world you swear
you're not a child of.
Every catalogue you open
lists early death for price.

I flip the light switch on.
Your eyes blink dreams back
for the showdown: a Socrates
hated unto hemlock, a Peter
crucified head-down for love. Already
I am one of the survivors.

A High Wind Through Your Life

for Istvan

A high wind blows through your life,
a boyhood rerunning the fields
and hills of Hungary
—a book hero's adventure for you—
vaulting over Austrian wire
while troops searched the village
for survivors.
                    In school
you were a rift in the regime,
the strange language
piling up in your thoughts.
Your mind wore a yellow star
for flight, rucksacks packed
in the closet, thinning gruel
and blankets—reminders nailed in
at every family gathering.
                        Your father
recounted the vanished names,
numbers so final
they left traces in the veins.
Teachers gave you gold stars
for the story's faultless grammar.

Where, within this scattered inheritance,
did you acquire your joy?
Not from the dropping away
of extra names, the everyday face
you put on for your daughters,
not from exiled memories
looking for the old addresses
in the homeland of your listening.

Moment by moment, you must forget,
you say, the star that crossed your past
with such foreign scintillation,
give love its safe-conduct.
                         Then you know
why wind speaks its high mind
in your blood, why physicians
need not justify the healer's vigil
when they lie awake, counting boxcars
on the first trains from the front.

Leaving the Conservatory

for David, aged 17, drowned in Mystic Lake

The more we look, the farther you recede
from your own, late face. The relinquished
form dissolves to a shimmer under
the surface the embalmer fixed. It's we
who surrender now to sleep as if in pond
weed dipping and rising like sorrow's
unheeded warnings, we who drift off
from the rented reverend's limp, rote
comfort as if from moorings too frail
to secure the whole weight of the truth.
Those who freight back and sort
the belongings—sour notes, clashes
of emotion, the final glorious riffs
under a studio moon; those who pay
everything, as one has to for a child;
they greet the bearers with pale smiles
and the darkening of years.

Meanwhile, you're the only one not here,
not whispering in the undertaker's
obligatory hush, the yellow explosion
of chrysanthemum. What we kneel before
is pillowed in a satin no real person's
heir to. It's more like the instrument
you laid aside, your oldest moment,
before you waded out—no swimmer—
past shore pines just starting
to reach for the first blue notes
of thrush, first light glinting
off green's topmost staffs.

Hard Beauty

You know the veils that come down
over eyes when the love's gone.
You know what it's like to walk out
for the last time, vanish
on the other side of the rain.
You've even practiced what dying
trees do, withdrawing the water
from their leaves. Did you forget
night lights don't go out
in the halls, even when it's late,
we're beat, and want to pinch off
the hot wicks of the candles?
Ask the long flocks
about the flyways of the heart.
Watch those who shore up nests
against the thaws, repeated frosts
of March, lengths of string streaming
from their chipped, determined beaks.
Remember how they suffer from a change
of trees. As for me, I'll be
a green day, no threats in it,
the pond under your eyelids
where the dream-fish dart,
an address book of vague promises,
precisely kept: Don't wait up.
If I search, I'll find you—
on the Sargasso Sea swells
of your lost love, or in the late,
drowned fields of the heart.
I, too, long for such hard beauty.

Photo of Myself Taken Near the
Mission Range,
Montana: Early Summer, 1974

A squinting interruption in an alfalfa foreground,
you pose in front of Herefords head-down
in their contentment.
                     My eyes move along
retreating barbed wire to the roughening
horizon: your future, blue and distant
as those hills—where what you hope
to synchronize your life with yields itself
like a green wind through your heart,
more than anyone who needed to halt
an instant in its frame could take.

I startle: a sharp wind off the cold plateau
gusts through me.
                What was you—the slight-
shouldered figure jolted from its stance
by the Nikon's click—blurs into a horizon
scarred and softened by the long-receded ice.
I learn its glacial patience,
surrender to the thaws and freezes
of alien terrain, my face capitulating
to its corrugations, the high country sun's
clear blue demands:
                  Under my feet
the cattle track, alfalfa battling
a labyrinth of roots, the prairie easing
endlessly away like a considerate lover.
Across the horizon, the barbed wire
quivers with premonitions.

Notes
Sierra Walk

Ollantaitambo (the name means "Fertile Field") was one of the major agricultural centers of the late Inca Empire, and also boasted some of the finest examples of Inca stone masonry outside of Cuzco. Many of the fitted-stone hill terraces constructed at that time are still used for growing maize and potatoes by the Quechua people—whom the Spanish of European descent contemptuously refer to as "cholos."

Indian Woman on Socabaya Street

The silver mines of Potosi were exploited for four centuries by the Spanish conquerors of Bolivia, and were legendary for their seemingly inexhaustible supplies of the precious ore. After the mine was depleted in the nineteenth century, however, tin—mined and sorted by native Aymara laborers—continued to enrich the mine owners, descendants of the original colonists.

THE AUTHOR

Carolyne Wright received her Master's and Doctorate in English and Creative Writing from Syracuse University, where she was awarded the Academy of American Poets Prize for 1977. She held a 1980-81 Writing Fellowship at the Fine Arts Work Center in Provincetown; a 1981 New York State C.A.P.S. Grant in Poetry; and received the 1981 Pablo Neruda Prize in Poetry from *Nimrod* Magazine. She has taught at Syracuse and Saint Lawrence Universities, and is currently Assistant Professor of Creative Writing at William Jewell College. Her previous publications are *Stealing the Children* (Ahsahta Press, Boise State University, 1978), now in a third printing; and a chapbook, *Returning What We Owed* (Owl Creek Press, 1980). Her poems, translations from the Spanish, and reviews have appeared in *Poetry, American Poetry Review, Iowa Review,* and *Ms.* Magazine, among others; and she is presently working on a memoir of the year she spent in Chile (1971-72) on a Fulbright-Hays Grant.

Ms. Wright in **Premonitions** is interested in those things just beyond the edge of our sensory perception, those things caught forever just in the corner of the eye. Her character Eulene is a subterranian part of self. Yet there is no lack of wry and pungent humor in these poems.

—Karen Swenson